STEM Book 1
Introduction

Safe in Cyberspace

Our STEMspiration

Lunabelle,
May your love for science continue to grow as you grow.

Cassandra-Jadel,
May you always be inspired to create, design, and build.

Maximilian   Dean the Mouse

Our STEMindset

Welcome to the world of *Max and the Mouse*. Before you read this book, we'd like to tell you about this unique project.

Who are Max and Dean?
Maximilian "Max" is a studious cat and half of a loveable team of adventurers. Max's best friend is Dean the mouse, and he is no ordinary mouse. Dean transforms, along with Max, each time they travel into cyberspace.

Why we created Max and The Mouse?
We hope to encourage young learners to explore SCIENCE, TECHNOLOGY, ENGINEERING, and MATHEMATICS, knowing that the future needs STEM subject experts. We want to invite educators and parents to use this book as a teaching tool.

What to expect?
Readers will notice portions of the book are in black and white and STEM related parts are in color. Embedded throughout the story for extra learning opportunities are quick resource Pawlinks. These Pawlinks can be opened by a QR scanning app once downloaded onto a mobile device.

When do the QR Pawlinks get scanned?

These resources can be viewed before, during, or after reading. We have found it helpful to read through the book one time before scanning the QR Pawlinks. They are considered an enhancement to the content of the book. QR Pawlinks provide definitions, graphics, and videos and can provide multiple opportunities for additional teaching and learning. At the end of this book your child or student will have the opportunity to receive a Cybercitizen Certificate.

Where should you read it?

Young students can enjoy this book while at school or at home. Books may also be read together with a parent or teacher that has a mobile device to scan Max's Pawlinks.

We look forward to captivating your hearts as you explore cyberspace adventures with Max and his mouse Dean.

Sincerely,

FAM Books

This is Maximilian.

He is a really smart cat.
Max reads lots of **STEM** books.
The **STEM** subjects are his favorite.

What are Acronyms?

STEM is an acronym for
SCIENCE, **TECHNOLOGY**, **ENGINEERING**, and **MATHEMATICS**.

Max likes to do **SCIENCE** experiments.
He uses his **ENGINEERING** and **MATH** skills to build robots.
Max dreams of building a rover and exploring Mars in it.

TECHNOLOGY is Max's favorite **STEM** subject.
He uses computers and mobile devices to access the Internet.

On the Internet Max can do research for school projects, chat and share pictures on social media websites, and play games in cyberspace.

What is the Internet?

Max has a special computer mouse.

This is Dean.

What is Cyberspace?

Dean and Max are best friends, and they travel into cyberspace together.

Max loves his adventures with Dean.
Dean is a superior cyberspace navigator.

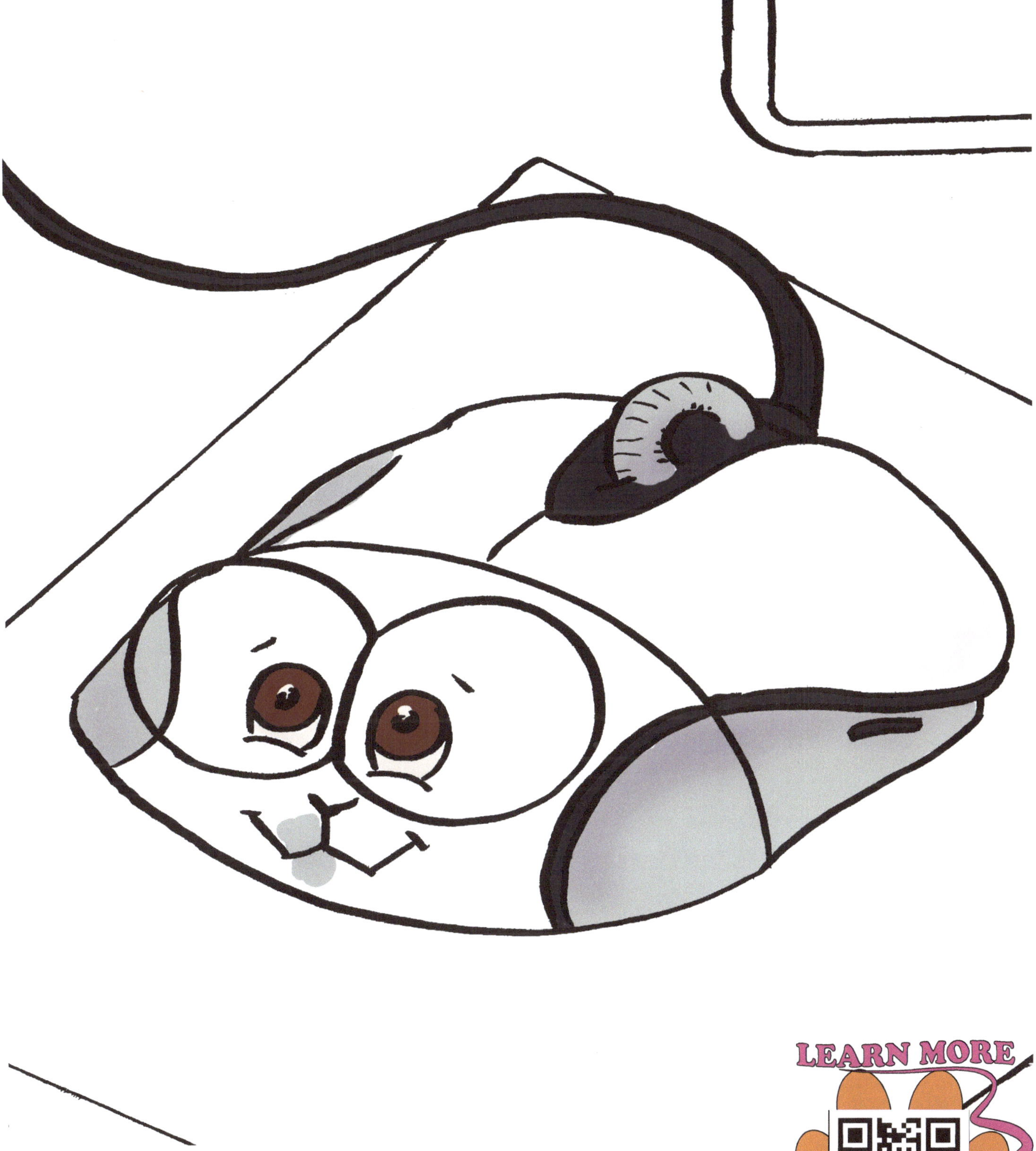

Dean helps Max learn while staying safe.

What is a Navigator?

Before they log on to the Web,
Dean reminds Max about the rules every good cybercitizen should follow.

"Thanks, Dean. Don't worry! I'm always a good cybercitizen…
I know the ABC's."

Explore the Web

"The First Rule: **A** stands for **Act Safely**," says Max.

Max types in his user name and stares at the password text box.
"I promise I'll keep my password a secret."

Dean responds, "Yes, and it should always be unique, so that no one can figure it out."

Protect your password

"To **Act Safely** is the best way to ensure cybersecurity," says Dean.

"If someone knows your password, they could steal your identity and pretend to be you."

LEARN MORE
Cybersecurity

"Oh no!" says Max. "They could ruin my high score on my Captain Catlastic game."
"Yes, that is true, and they can do a lot more damage to your identity and security," warns Dean.

"A good way to protect yourself is to create a strong password.
Make sure it's something that no one can guess.
Use a combination of upper and lowercase letters, numbers, and symbols.
For example, **Cheese4ME!** is a great 10-digit password."

Dean points to the screen and lines up the cursor, "Alright, Maximilian, logging on."

Max smiles, "Ready, Set,... CLICK!!!"
And in a blink of an eye, Max and Dean lunge safely into cyberspace!

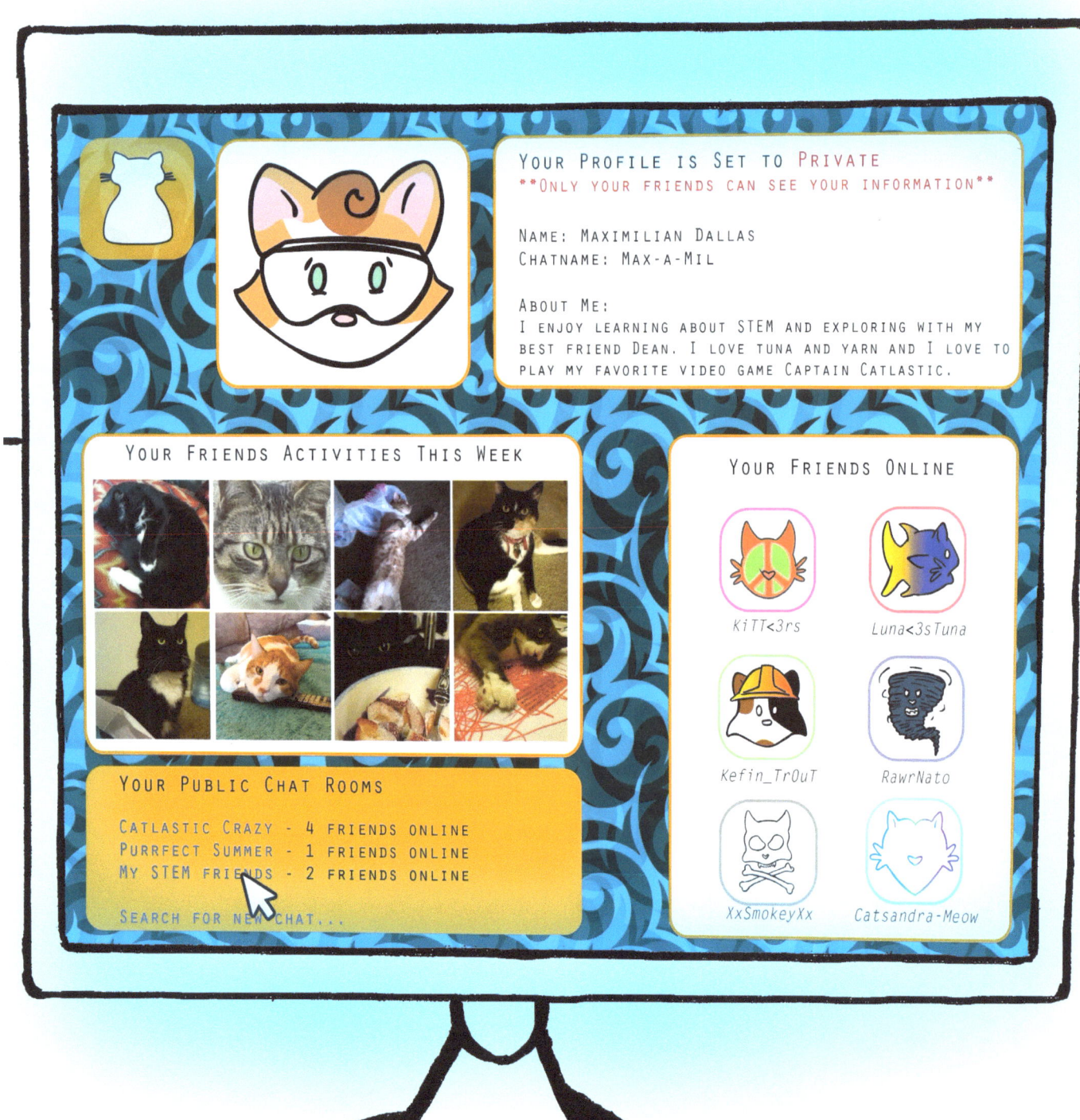

Max and Dean find themselves in their favorite social media website "SnapCat," where Max chats with his online friends.

Maximilian has entered the chat room

XxSmokeyXx: Hey

KiTT<3rs: Hi

XxSmokeyXx: 😼

MaX-a-MiL: Hi Everyone

KiTT<3rs: Hey Max! Whacha been up to??

MaX-a-MiL: I went on a field trip with school yesterday.

XxSmokeyXx: Where did you go?

MaX-a-MiL: The Cannery!

KiTT<3rs: Meow, What's The Cannery?

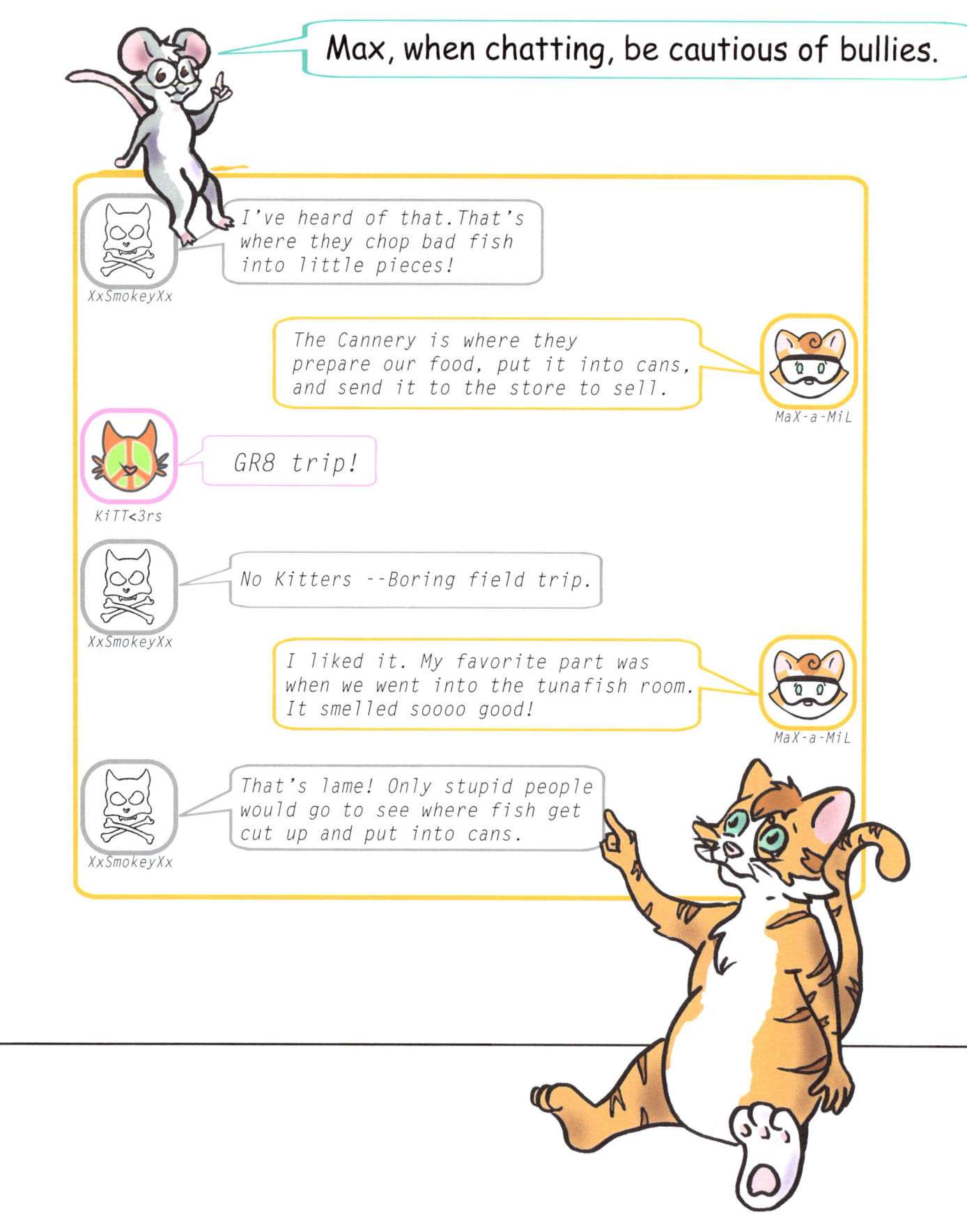

Behave Respectfully

Smokey is not following the second rule - **Behave Respectfully**.

He doesn't have good netiquette.

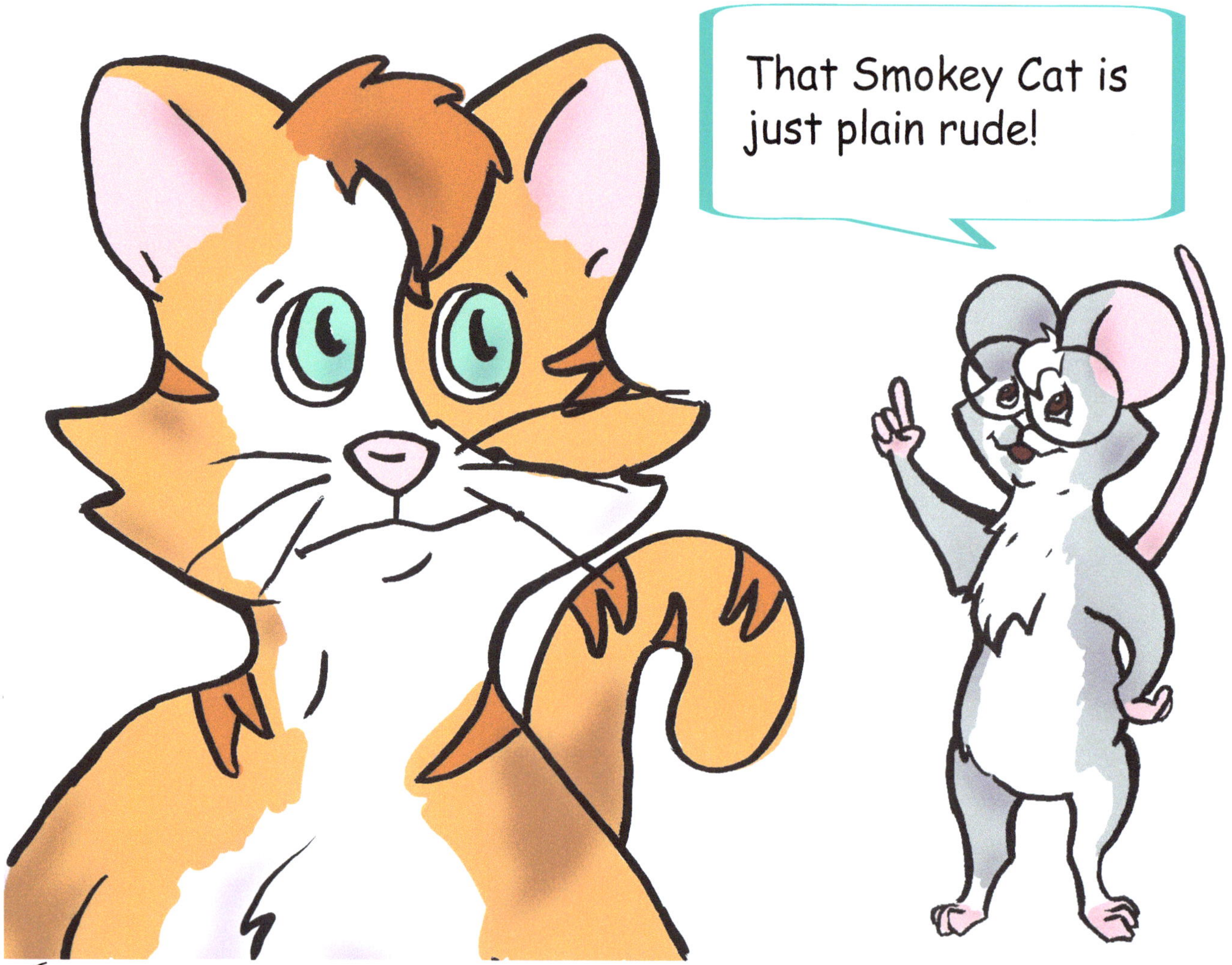

Digital Etiquette "Netiquette"

That Smokey Cat is just plain rude!

KiTT<3rs

That's not very nice Smokey.

KiTT<3rs

Max isn't stupid, and his opinion is just as important as mine or yours.

XxSmokeyXx

I have a better field trip idea...
www.virtual-tour/catatonic/poison-fish.com

*Stop Kitters!
Don't click on that link!
You could download a virus!*

MaX-a-MiL

Good advice, Max!

You remembered the third cybercitizenship Rule

- **Choose Responsibly!**

Never click on a strange link or download without an adult.

"I'm Out. This is a waste of my time."

Smokey has left the chat room

"Yikes, I'm glad he left! He wasn't a good cybercitizen."

"Smokey didn't have a clue about the ABC's."

"Bullying is mean and cyberbullying is very hard to stop because it's in the virtual world, not the physical world," reminds Dean.

Cyberbullying

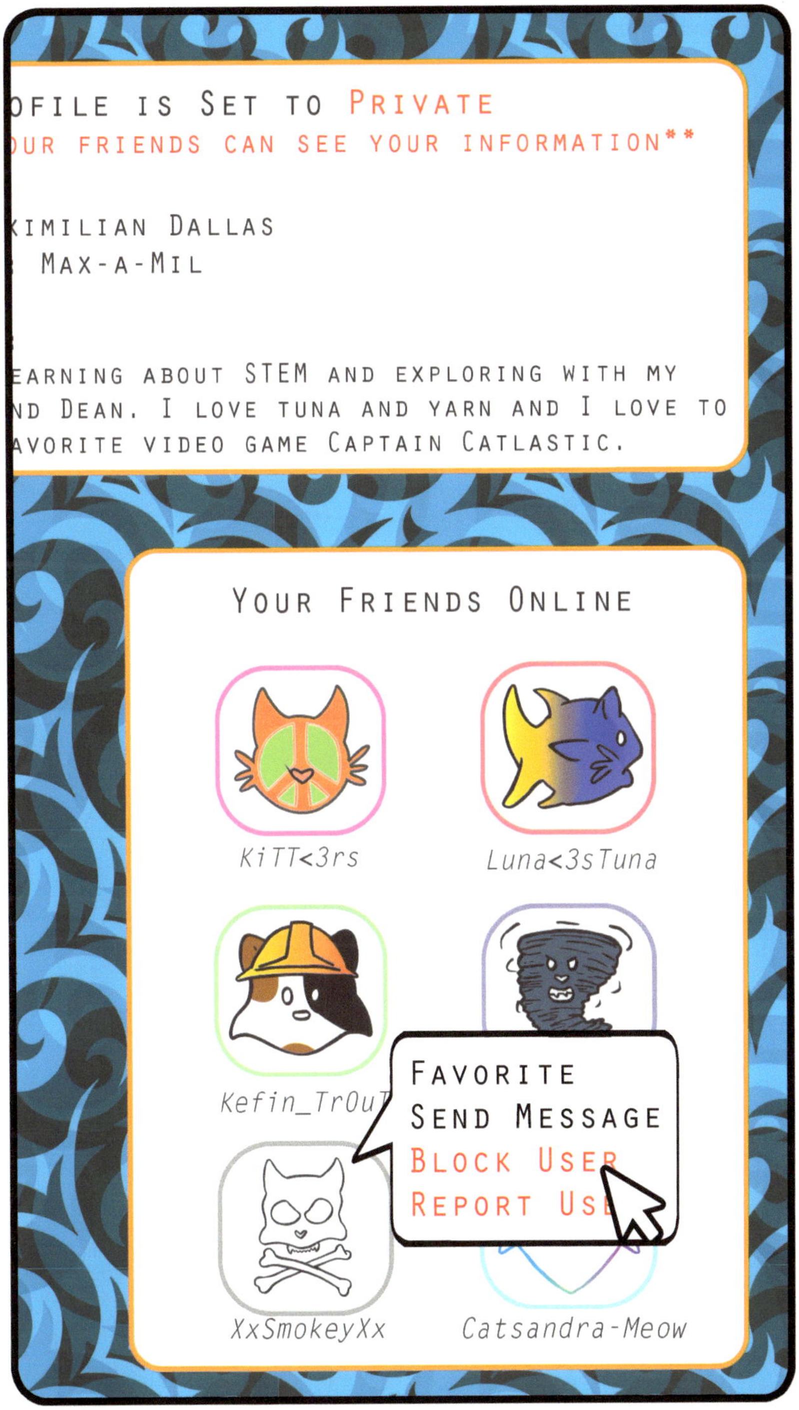

"Never, ever communicate with someone who is a <u>cyberbully.</u> We will go into your profile, block Smokey from chatting with us, and report his bad behavior."

"Dean, take a screenshot of our chat. I want to show it to my mom. I'll tell her that I blocked Smokey and reported him."

"Great Idea Max!" Click - Screenshot Saved!

"It is also important to make sure your account is set to private and not public, otherwise anyone could see your information."

MaX-a-MiL: I blocked Smokey and took screenshots to use when I report him.

KiTT<3rs: Meowerzs! I will too. He had bad energy.

MaX-a-MiL: LOL

KiTT<3rs: So, Where is The Cannery? I wanna go! We should go together sometime.

MaX-a-MiL: It's close to my house.

KiTT<3rs: Where do you live? I live in Dogtown. This is one of my favorite photos of me in front of my house...

"Stop, Max. Wait!" Dean stops Max from chatting.
"You know that giving personal information isn't <u>safe</u> on the Internet?"

"Yeah, I know. Kitters is my friend though," replies Max.

"Don't forget, **Act Safely!** Never give information about where you live or specific details about yourself such as your address, age, last name, or even your school," warns Dean.
"Kitters just posted her address in that photo and, she's asking for yours."

"Dean, this isn't Stranger-Danger! Kitters is a friend," says Max.

"Max, Internet safety includes your conversations with friends. Once you put it on the internet, it is there forever. You never know who might see it!"

"Yikes, Dean, okay! I won't send personal information. I've got it."

Internet Safety

*Wait Kitters!
It's important to Act Safely in cyberspace.
We shouldn't chat about personal information,
like where we live.*

*We need to follow the Cybercitizen ABC's and
Act Safely, Behave Respectfully,
and Choose Responsibly.
If we want to go together to The Cannery,
we should have our moms plan it.*

 *Meowzers!? I never thought about safety rules in cyberspace!*

 *Also, It isn't safe to post pictures without our parent's approval. For example, did you know that the one you posted has your house number on it?*

MaX-a-MiL

 *OMG! It does? I'll delete it. Thank you, Max, you're a good friend!*

KiTT<3rs

 *Well, I better Choose Responsibly and logoff for dinner now!*

KiTT<3rs

KiTT<3rs

MaX-a-MiL

"Thanks for all your help, Dean. I'm ready to go home. Being a good cybercitizen has made me hungry and tired."

Dean agrees, "That could have been a catastrophe, but your cybersmarts were out of this world today!
Great job following the ABC's of cybercitizenship!"

After Max and Dean leave cyberspace, Max eats dinner with his mom and tells her about his adventures.

After dinner, Max climbs into bed.
"Thanks, Dean. That was fun. I'm ready for a long catnap now."

"Good idea. I think I'll go into sleep mode myself."

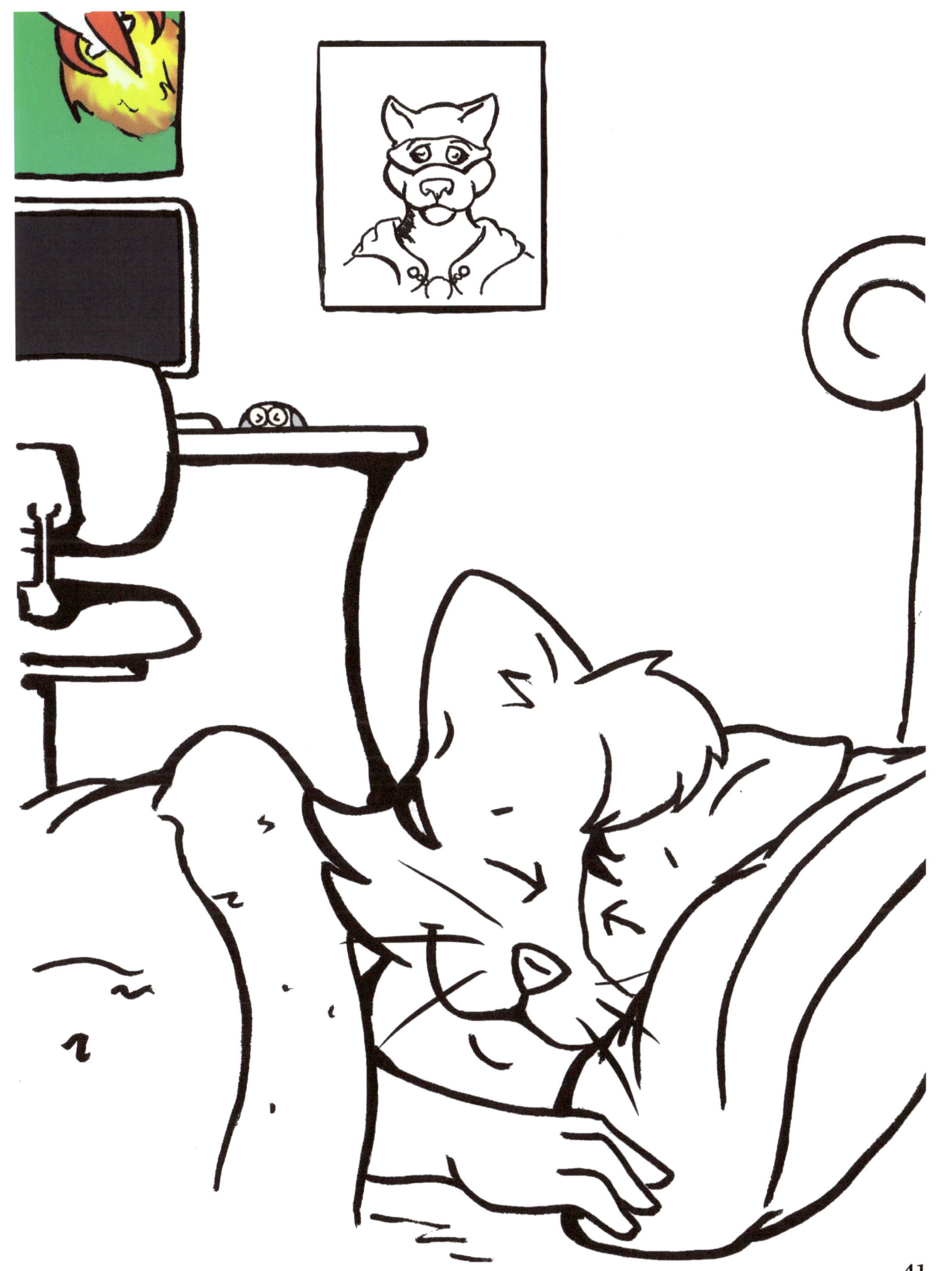

Cybercitizen Certificate

Congratulations! Now that you have the knowledge to begin your journey as a Cybercitizen, Max and Dean invite you to take the ABC pledge and print out your certificate.

Pledge and Certificate

Join the FAM club

Our FAM fans are the first to hear about new adventures, offers, and the latest information about your favorite characters and **STEM** topics.

FAM Fan Club

Meet Our FAM Creators

This book was creatively developed by FAM Books. We are one family, Franklin, Armentrout, Moreira (FAM); mom, daughter-in-law, and daughter.

Kimberly Franklin, Author

Kimberly Franklin has worked in the field of education for over 20 years. Her career includes positions as Public Educator and Administrator, Program Manager for Disney Institute, Curriculum Designer for Laureate Education, and K-12 STEM Learning Expert for NASA's Department of Education.

Justine Armentrout, Illustrator

Justine Armentrout has her degree in environmental science and is a **STEM** advocate. She is a champion for the rights of animals and has a passion for health and personal wellness. Justine is a talented artist and has worked on multiple projects bringing the inanimate to life.

Elizabeth Moreira, Design and Layout

Elizabeth Moreira has a Bachelor of Science in Design and creates specialty business and event marketing materials, graphic, and environmental design pieces. She is an accomplished leader in the hospitality industry and professional development facilitator.

She is a mother of 2 **STEM**inded daughters.

Our STEMsources

Max and The Mouse would like to thank the following sources used in our QR Pawlinks and for providing additional resources for our families:

ABCya!

www.abcya.com

Video QRs

http://www.abcya.com/ Cyber-Five video, http://www.abcya.com/cyber_five_internet_safety.htm

BrainPOP

www.brainpop.com

Video QRs

https://www.brainpop.com/technology/freemovies/digitaletiquette/

Common Sense Media

www.commonsensemedia.org

Providing information for families on internet privacy and safety

https://www.commonsensemedia.org/lists/kid-safe-browsers-and-search-sites
https://www.commonsensemedia.org/videos/5-internet-safety-tips-for-kids
https://www.commonsensemedia.org/videos/5-ways-to-stop-cyberbullies-0
www.commonsensemedia.org/privacy-and-internet-safety/how-do-i-protect-my-kids

Khan Academy

"NOTE: All Khan Academy content is available for free at www.khanacademy.org".

Video QRs

https://www.khanacademy.org/computing/computer-science/internet-intro/internet-works-intro/v/the-internet-wires-cables-and-wifi

https://www.khanacademy.org/partner-content/nova/cybersecurity/cyber/v/cybersecurity-101

https://www.khanacademy.org/computing/computer-programming/html-css/intro-to-html/v/making-webpages-intro

https://www.khanacademy.org/computing/computer-science/internet-intro/internet-works-intro/v/the-internet-cybersecurity-and-crime

Kids Wordsmyth

Definition QRs

https://kids.wordsmyth.net/we/

NASA JPL Caltech

Posters and Content QRs

https://marsmobile.jpl.nasa.gov/multimedia/resources/mars-posters-explorers-wanted/